Summary of Fire and Fury: Inside the Trump White House

By

Michael Wolff

SpeedyReads

Note to readers:

This is a SpeedyReads guide to Michael Wolff's "Fire and Fury: Inside the Trump White House" meant to enhance your reading experience. You are encouraged to buy the original book.

Copyright 2017. All rights reserved. No part of this publication may be reproduced, stored in a retrieval system or transmitted in any form or by any means, electronic, mechanical, photocopying, recording or otherwise, without prior permission of the publisher.

Limit of Liability / Disclaimer of Warranty: The publisher and author make no representations or warranties with respect or the accuracy or completeness of these contents and disclaim all warranties such as warranties of fitness of a particular purpose. The author or publisher are not liable for any damages whatsoever. The fact that an individual or organization is referred to in this document as a citation or source of information does not imply that the author or publisher endorses the information that the individual or organization provided. This is an unofficial summary & analytical review and has not been approved by the original author of the book.

Your Free Gift

As a way of saying "thank you" for your purchase, We're offering you a free special report that's *exclusive* for our book readers.

In **"Delicious Reading: How to Quadruple and Enhance Your Book Reading Experience Within 24 Hours"**, you'll discover simple but powerful ways to heighten and enhance your book reading experience that was only known by the top book connoisseurs…. Until now…

Go to the link below before it expires!

http://www.easysummaries.com/gift

Summary of Fire and Fury: Inside the Trump White House

Contents

Your Free Gift

Summary of Fire and Fury: Inside the Trump White House

Summary of Fire and Fury

- Chapter 1
- Chapter 2
- Chapter 3
- Chapter 4
- Chapter 5
- Chapter 6
- Chapter 7
- Chapter 8
- Chapter 9
- Chapter 10
- Chapter 11
- Chapter 12
- Chapter 13
- Chapter 14
- Chapter 15
- Chapter 16
- Chapter 17

Chapter 18

Chapter 19

Chapter 20

Chapter 21

Chapter 22

Background Information about Fire and Fury

Background Information About Michael Wolff

Books by Michael Wolff

Discussion Questions on Fire and Fury

Do you want special deals?

FINAL SURPRISE BONUS

Summary of Fire and Fury

Chapter 1

On the 8th of November, 2016, Kellyanne Conway, Donald Trump's campaign manager, was not concerned about Trump's looming defeat despite being sure of it. She considered the inevitable defeat to be Reince Priebus's fault rather than hers. In addition to Priebus, she also held his sidekick Katie Walsh and Sean Spicer accountable for the upcoming. She was looking forward to a career in TV. Everyone including Trump and Jared Kushner was sure of the outcome of the election. The only person who thought Trump would actually win was Steve Bannon but no one believed him. In simple words, Trump and those in his campaign were prepared to lose but not prepared to win. Further, Trump's financial contribution to the campaign had been only lending $10 million on the promise that he would get it back.

Also, Melania Trump and Trump spent hardly any time together. Trump thought he had mastered the art of marriage the third time by living and letting live. Before Trump ran for president, Melania thought he would win. However, Melania was extremely hurt by the whisper campaign about her that began after Trump's nomination, especially after the leak of an old nude photo-shoot. When it became evident that Trump was winning that day, it shocked Trump, Melania and many others.

Chapter 2

Rupert Murdoch came extremely late to a gathering at Trump Tower on the Saturday after the election and every passing minute made Trump restless. Murdoch considered Trump to be a fool. Apart from Murdoch, many other billionaires had also paid little attention to Trump prior to his victory but now had to think again. It was time for Trump to form the government. People like Jim Mattis, Rex Tillerson, Scott Pruitt and Betsy DeVos joined despite their early impressions of Trump. However, it was becoming increasingly clear to those joining the government that Trump hardly knew anything.

A close Trump friend found Trump and Bill Clinton quite similar, including their womanizing personalities. One of Trump's characteristics is that he liked to sleep with his friends' wives by tricking his friends into compromising situations and letting their wives hear about their thoughts.

Even after winning, Trump was not aware of the basic requirements of the job since he lacked any capacity to plan, arrange, concentrate and shift. Trump did not understand the needs and delicate nature of the job of a chief of staff and wanted to give it to family. He had to be informed that it could not happen. Chris Christie was also considered for the job. However, Christie had to be removed from Trump's orbit because of his unfavorable history with Jared Kushner's father. The next name on the list was Steve Bannon but a lot of people resisted it because of his disorganized ways and other reasons. Therefore, Reince Priebus landed the job. Trump was further under the illusion that the tech industry needed him and Murdoch considered him an idiot for it.

Chapter 3

Between election and inauguration, Jared Kushner acquired the status of an interconnection between Trump and the establishment. People offered advice and warnings to him to pass to Trump. They also informed him about the necessary nature of making nice with the intelligence community, which Trump had targeted considerably in the course of his campaign. Jared Kushner decided to tell Trump to reach out to the CIA first.

Trump was already angry on the day of his inauguration, since several stars had refused to be part of his big day. He fought with Melania throughout that morning. In addition, the crowd did not live up to his expectations and this is why his Bannon-composed speech sounded upset. However, by the next morning, his optimism had returned and he had fabricated the strength of the crowd and repeated it during his conversations with friends and others. This paved the way for a norm of the Trump administration to be established i.e. alternative versions of realities and the infamous terms Kellyanne Conway used to defend Trump i.e. 'alternative facts,' which was supposed to be presented as 'alternative information.'

Trump met the CIA and his meeting with the CIA somehow left them lost for words for some time because of the 'Trump' way he handled.

Chapter 4

Bannon's role as Trump's Chief Strategist was his first formal political job. After the transition, Bannon became even more focused and intense than ever, which left many bewildered. He was focusing on the new goal of reaching further heights in his political ambitions. A lot of people felt then that he was plotting against them. Some points to note about Bannon indicate that he was not particularly successful as an entrepreneur, had failed marriages and was not really a nice person. Bannon was determined to change the way of the government since he was here for revenge. He discovered that executive orders were the way to make things real.

Further, Sean Spicer could not do his job of explicating why and what people did in the administration since no one had a job or did it. Further, Bannon had Stephen Miller draft the immigration executive order (EO). When the travel ban was signed and took immediate effect, it led to an outcry. However, Bannon felt content since he had managed to give rise to a boundary between Trump's America and that of the liberals. He did it on a Friday so that the liberals would go to the airports, protest and seem crazy.

Chapter 5

When *Morning Joe* hosts Joe Scarborough and Mika Brzezinski visited the White House, Trump asked them how his first week had gone, expecting adulation. Joe changed the subject. Trump brought it up again and Joe mentioned the immigration order and how it seemed like a rough span. Trump responded humorously.

Bannon had coined the Jarvanka conflation to refer to Jared and Ivanka. When Trump became president, it was an unexpected turn of events and like everyone else, Jared and Ivanka also wanted to capitalize on it. They made a deal that that if opportunity arose, it would be Ivanka who would run for president to become the first ever female president. When Bannon heard about this deal, he could not believe it.

In addition, the reason Jared became part of the White House was to have leverage owing to the proximity to the president. Ivanka's public meeting with Dina Powell at Four Seasons, someone Ivanka helped enter the White House, showed the world that Trump's family was enthusiastic about the power structure.

Chapter 6

During the early weeks of Trump's presidency, it became apparent to Trump's friends that he was neither being presidential nor considering his new position and controlling his behavior. His tweets continued, he did not want to adhere to scripted remarks and his calls to his friends, full of self-pity, kept coming. This arose from the fact that like other presidents, he had not had to take a leap or go through a major transformation since he already came from a position of privilege.

Moreover, Trump deviated from the norm in his daily White House life and ordered a lock on his White House bedroom, to the dismay of the Secret Service who wanted access to the room. His new rules included no one touching anything, especially his toothbrush. He had a fear of being poisoned and this was why he loved McDonald's since no one knows he is coming and the food is already made. He forbade anyone from changing the sheets without being asked by him. Trump's schedule in his room was based on having cheeseburgers, watching TV and calling people. He usually went to bed early. After the bathrobe news, he has always denied wearing a bathrobe and was angry at the media for delving too deeply into his personal life.

However, after the difficult start, things improved with Trump's nomination of Neil Gorsuch to the Supreme Court, which was well received.

Trump had first wanted to nominate a friend but settled for Gorsuch.

Chapter 7

The Russia story was an attempt to implicate Trump's presidency in a scandal since nothing else was working. From Kellyanne Conway to Sean Spicer, everyone reacted to it differently. As far as Bannon was concerned, he dismissed it as a conspiracy theory. As a result of their investigation, the CIA, FBI and NSA concluded the existence of an influence campaign initiated by Vladimir Putin to target the U.S. presidential election. Trump's senior staff was more concerned about the shady business dealings of Trump and Kushner. When news got out on Michael Flynn's link with Russia, Trump was still not convinced to let go of him but eventually agreed to fire him. It is evident that those close to Trump were concerned all the time about the media, what it was reporting and what was getting leaked. Most of them adopted a policy of not saying anything about the Russia scandal unless absolutely necessary.

Chapter 8

After some weeks, Steve Bannon realized that White House was actually a military facility. However, Trump's presidency was as far from the military brand of discipline as possible. There was chaos everywhere, people came and went, and every individual wanted to attend each meeting. In addition, the lack of good management was evident from the detail that if something happened in Trump's absence, he did not care about it at all. The initial days of Trump's presidency made it clear that Priebus, Kushner and Bannon were all battling to take charge of the White House and be the actual power. Add Trump to it, who wanted to keep all power. Katie Walsh, the deputy chief of staff, was stuck in the middle of it all.

Walsh was a personification of a specific Republican ideal and a true bureaucrat. She was a true political figure amidst everything, and at the heart of running things. She realized that the essence of the campaign was lost after the Trump team shifted to the White House. Walsh expressed that trying to guess what Trump was thinking was like attempting to guess what a child wants. Since Trump did not read or even skim, some considered him to be semiliterate. Since he could read headlines about himself and gossip, there were divided opinions. Some believed him to be dyslexic; others considered him to be postliterate - completely TV. Also, he did not even listen.

Still, what gave hope to people like Walsh and others was the thought that Trump could not have become the president without fundamental cunning and knowing what he was doing. However, meetings told a different story since Trump did not seem to want anything to do with third-party information. In addition to the battle between Priebus, Kushner and Bannon, it was also an issue that Mike Pence seemed like the weakest vice president in decades.

Chapter 9

On the 23rd of February, the West Wing was excited about the Conservative Political Action Conference (CPAC). Richard Spencer, the president of the National Policy Institute and someone considered to be a think tank pertaining to white supremacists, also attempted to attend CPAC but was denied an entrance. Spencer compared Trump to Hitler and became famous for 'Hail Trump.' On the other hand, Kushner felt taunted by Bannon's CPAC speech when he heard it and the speech enraged him considerably. Trump's CPAC speech satisfied Spencer.

Chapter 10

Jarvanka had grown wary of the White House leaks by now. Kushner was sure Bannon would not stop at anything to destroy them. He had also come to the conclusion that Bannon was an anti-Semite. Kushner further considered Bannon's right-wing defense of Israel as a twisted form of anti-Semitism aimed at him. So he responded by adding his own tough-guy Jews to the White House i.e. Goldman Jews. This brought Gary Cohn to the picture. Dina Powell also became part of this Jarvanka-Gary camp. Trump's speech to the joint session of Congress on the 28th of February provided this camp a chance to exclude Bannon. Ivanka, with the assistance of her camp, drafted the speech. The speech helped Trump get good reviews and transformed his presidency's tone. This also declared a new West Wing brain trust.

Chapter 11

The media and Trump never became good friends and the only reason that young Hope Hicks was so adored by Trump was her continued efforts to bring the news to Trump in a reasonable manner; in a fashion where Trump had not committed a huge tragedy in any manner. It was due to Hicks that Trump never understood why his association with the Russians, exposed by a previous employee of the white house administration, was a disastrous event. Trump thought that his attorney general was the cause of this issue and tried to cook up something to remove his attorney general.

On the other hand, there was a new rumor brewing in the white house, thanks to Tony Blair.

Tony Blair provided Jared with the possibility that the connections might have been drawn out of possible spying on Trump during his days of campaigning for Presidential elections. It was later with Blair's interview that Trump's fears were confirmed that the Obama administration did indeed hate him and he was innocently caught in their web of lies. Obama's officials, for their part, denied any such rumor while Trump continued on his social media rant whereby he became even more of a clown for the general public.

Chapter 12

Trump, while promising things during his campaign, had not realized how serious the situation was going to be and how he was expected to know things and pass laws/policies when he himself did not have an ounce of understanding about the topics. Obamacare was one such instance where his political alliance with the Republicans required him to take care of the law and modify it for better while he himself was not interested in the issue. Paul Ryan came in to play at this time. While Ryan was hated by Bannon because of their political history with each other during the campaign period, Bannon himself couldn't do a thing to stop his influence. Ryan had openly objected to Trump and Bannon before and now he turned a new leaf to remain in his seat of power.

FBI Director James Comey at this time surfaced as a new enemy of Trump and his family. Before the Russian debacle, the Trump family had had no issues with Comey but the issues started for the worse. Bannon, on the other hand, saw that this intrusion by FBI would result in the decline of Jared Kushner as he was involved in it and so he asked people to grab popcorns for the coming show.

Chapter 13

Bannon was slowly but surely coming to a conclusion that there was a propaganda going on against him within the administration at the White House. Bannon, whose views were seen by the political right as ideals and what was considered initially the very roots of Trump's campaigning, were being eroded by the works and influence of Jared and Ivanka. While Bannon considered that he and the president were well-aligned in their consideration over what is the future of America, Trump was learning a new language that demeaned Bannon for the smallest of things.

Ivanka and Jared, on the other hand, were given power in the system by their appointments and this was seen by Bannon and his supporters as a takeover of the administration by those with Trump's blood ties. The duo reportedly pushed for the end of Bannon's position in the White House but the Mercers helped Bannon in retaining some amount of dignity through their own influence in the White House. However, it should be remembered that Bannon was no longer the person that made Trump happy. Rather, Trump started getting irritated with him, while Ivanka and Kushner saw an improvement in their position to a level where Trump would listen to and accept whatever they said to him.

Chapter 14

Next came a change in world politics that no one was anticipating this quickly but was something that was inevitable; an attack in Syria by the Assad government by chemical weapons. While this attack would be considered by many as a serious event, the president had seemingly no interest in the event, not even an attention span that would allow him to feel sorry for the distressed nation and pay his respects to the dead.

Ivanka and Jared, on the other hand, were stressed by the route taken by the president, and it was at this point that many came to recognize Powell and Cohn for what they were i.e. assets. Ivanka and Powell worked hard to find a way to get the president to sympathize because Bannon's opposition to involvement in a foreign country's matters was making more sense to Trump. H.R. McMaster, member of the National Security Council, failed to get the point of importance of the Syrian conflict across to Trump. Thankfully, it was Ivanka's memory of how her father's brain worked that helped save face. Trump liked easy pictures and that was how the point got through to him. This point resulted in a missile attack on Syria's airport, something that was not appreciated by Bannon.

Chapter 15

The media favoring the political left hates what the media supporting the political right reports and vice versa. While the more intelligent crowd would understand this statement, Trump certainly could not do so. Trump, in his naivety, considered the attacks from the liberal media as personal rather than political and this point soon came to dictate how the politics within the White House started to roll.

Conway, for her part, became the best friend that Trump would need to succeed since even though she didn't like what Trump said, she still presented it to the world. On the other hand, Hicks became Trump's hope for good press but regardless of her tries to give Trump just that, she continued to fail. Trump cannot ever ignore the media and since he cannot do so, he continued to try to make them happy and that is something that can never be accomplished.

With the White House correspondent dinner soon to happen, Trump was extremely enthusiastic about the possibilities of good press even though whole of his administration was scared of the possible massacre. It was ultimately Bannon who got through to Trump and got him away from the event, stating that Trump did not need to be an 'extra' for the nemesis.

Chapter 16

Comey came under Trump's proverbial microscope following the case where the justice department started taking an initiative with regards to Trump's electoral win and the connection with Russia. While the issue with Trump and Russia would have soon disappeared from the newsstands, the importance of this issue became greatly emphasized due to the Kushner family ties with the Russia issue. Jared's family had business obligations to the Chinese and at the same time, were friends with an Israeli who had Russian affiliations. Trump further hyperbolized the relation in front of different audiences.

Trump and his family wanted to end Comey's career and they did so with the most baseless issues rather than showing that it was due to FBI's nosing into family business. Bannon and Priebus, on the other hand, saw the position as what it really was, a train wreck; but the stance taken by these two had a more political pretext, which was their hatred towards the Kushners and Ivanka. Trump later stated that the reason for such a decision with regards to Comey was taken based on Rod Rosenstein's legal advice but that wasn't so and Rosenstein later showed his full resentment of the situation by appointing Robert Mueller as the new investigating power over Trump's family's Russia connections.

Chapter 17

Trump did not anticipate that the issue with Comey would continue to plague him as it later did and as a result, Bannon and Priebus gained their best evidence against Ivanka and Jared. They continued to ridicule every decision coming from the president that was fueled by Trump's favorite dynamic duo.

President Trump's understanding of foreign policy being nil, the initial contacts and alliances were gained by simple childish plans by the president whereby policy became a tit for tat game. Middle East being a point of interest for the previous presidencies, also became a target for Trump and he settled into the arena to right the wrongs of the world and attain the precious ceasefire. However, the policy resulted in a change in dynamics in the Middle East as the crown prince of Saudi Arabia was changed thanks to the Trump influence and no war was initiated with the likes of Qatar. Trump considered everything as a yes or no questionnaire and such was his opinion on the Israel-Palestine conflict.

Bannon, on the other hand, worked on the sideline to keep Trump president while simultaneously taking away his source of pleasure, the media, from the close parameter.

Chapter 18

Bannon felt that he had won his place back into Trump's office with the help of his well-placed comments made to the ear of the president. The reentry of Bannon felt like a threat to Trump's daughter and son-in-law since the two parties were opposing each other in everything they did and what they wanted to inspire from Trump. Bannon, for his part, started the operation to keep Trump away from serious politics to ensure that nothing controversial gets out and Trump agreed to the change.

Trump, on the other hand, became the target of countrywide loathing from the media thanks to the statements from Comey over how his condition of joblessness came to be. The differences between

Comey and Trump set the tone perfectly for the media as people came to learn that Trump was basically fooling around in his office while surrounded by his minders who tried and failed to keep him contained from various messes.

While Brannon was pushing for more space by ensuring that Ivanka and Jared were isolated from everyone including Trump, they held the view that the fall of Trump was coming as a consequence of Bannon's influence that was eroding Trump's usual disposition.

Chapter 19

MSNBC became a point of contention for Trump. As the media from that sector was once considered a close ally, how and why this association took turn for the worse could not be understood by Trump. Trump, on his end, still could not understand why he was not gaining popularity among the crowd as the media continued to mock his efforts in the White House. It was during the stressful period brought upon by the anchors at MSNBC that exposed the inadequacies of Trump and his government that Trump reacted in a manner that he usually does, by tweeting about the issue in a childish manner. Regardless of his position, Trump failed to grasp that politics required subtlety.

On the other hand, a previously hidden scandal of confirmed Russian and Trump family's association came to the limelight out of blue. The scandal brought to light that the Trumps simply failed to take the politics of America seriously even 6 months before the elections as they freely affiliated with the Russians just to fuel their mudslinging capacities.

On another end, the Comey and Mueller trouble was coming to the surface as the implications of untrustworthiness settled around the White House and public distrust with the officials heightened. The White House itself became a place of stress as a dividing line was drawn between those who caused the incident with Comey and those who did not.

Chapter 20

The situation with Afghanistan, a long standing and a useless war as seen by Bannon, came to a rise because Trump needed to make a decision with regards to this situation and the suggestions provided by the administration, specifically McMaster and then the ones provided by military journals, were not going to move the war to a point that Trump wanted. Trump wanted to do something new with the war issue and the options provided to him were not new, they were the same old and Trump despised old.

Ivanka and Jared were busy on their own end, to ensure that the war proceeded in a milder manner and so they backed McMaster in the way that they could, by making Bannon the target as they always had before and Bannon failed to realize the threat.

It was actually Ivanka and Jared that brought Anthony Scaramucci into the White House, as a political figure in the communication department. Scaramucci, on his end, was interested just to benefit from the tax issues in relation with his business. It was reportedly seen and felt that he was useless and untrustworthy because of his earlier lack of loyalty when Trump's campaign was going downhill.

Chapter 21

Bannon, in his narcissistic rants, revealed his strong disbelief in the placement of Scaramucci, calling him the biggest joke yet in the White House. White House's continued efforts to fight within itself and derail one another in front of the public, while at the same time trying to stop the fire(news) from spreading into the minds of the trusting voters, became a tiring routine that became a cycle. Bannon thought that his win in the Afghanistan decision was going to last and that was a bad prediction to make since he did not know what Trump was going to do next. On the other side of the spectrum, Jared's father's imprisonment brought in great joy to Bannon as he thought that this was going to be a decline of that business.

Scaramucci was promoted to a position above Bannon and Priebus by Trump, a move that ended the comedy of the situation. Scaramucci then went ahead to make Priebus redundant in a public expose in a newspaper. Trump being Trump showed some sympathy toward Priebus but it turned out that he was just bidding his time as he soon tweeted not only about firing Priebus but also about making a new hire to replace him, General Kelly.

Chapter 22

Michael Kelly, being in a position where he thought that he could place stoppers to the position held by Ivanka and Jared, thought he can place them in limits by shaking some sense into Trump. However, it turned out that Trump very much liked to be in alliance with his daughter and son-in-law. This was a problem that Bannon thought would end with Kelly's insistence. Bannon and Kelly hence came to another dead end with their try on getting the dynamic duo out of the Oval Office. Kelly did make it known that he would be the one who would decide whether or not their influence worked on Trump as they would have to go through him. However, this stance did not last thanks to the forceful intrusion by the dynamic duo.

Trump, having been told to work on his vacationing time, could not be expected to be sane ever and he showcased this aspect when he reacted to the issue of opioids, then the issue of bombing the North Korea was raised and then the final straw in the form of Charlottesville tragedy. As a result of his comments on the occasion, the public around the country came to fear Trump's mind and soon the company owners and executives that were following him blindly, stopped doing so.

Background Information about Fire and Fury

A huge number of questions and controversies surround the Trump presidency. Only a limited number of people thought it possible that Donald Trump would actually win the 2016 presidential election and yet he somehow did. Trump, who was a controversial figure even before winning, has not evaded controversy in the course of his presidency. *Fire and Fury: Inside the Trump White House* was published in January 2018. Author Michael Wolff underlines that he somehow acquired the status of a fly on the wall during the early weeks of Trump presidency after being given access by Trump as a result of a book suggestion by Wolff. The book resulted from what he saw and heard during this time and his conversations with people about Trump. The text presents an account of Trump's habits, behavior and thought processes as POTUS and the actions, thinking patterns and words of his staff at the White House. It also details the battle for power and dynamics between different forces, most importantly Steve Bannon, Ivanka Trump, Jared Kushner, Reince Priebus, etc. The book acquired the number one spot on New York Times' bestseller list. A lawyer for Trump attempted to halt its publication with cease-and-desist letters but to no avail. *Fire and Fury* has made some controversial revelations about Trump and those around him and is a much talked about affair.

Background Information About Michael Wolff

Michael Wolff enjoys the status of being a writer, journalist, columnist and essayist. He has contributed to several publications including the UK version of *GQ*, *USA Today*, *The Hollywood Reporter*, etc. He was the co-founder of the news aggregation website Newser and served as the editor of Adweek previously. He has written seven books and received a Mirror Award and two National Magazine Awards

Books by Michael Wolff

☐ *White Kids. 1979.*

☐ *Where We Stand: Can America Make It in the Global Race for Wealth, Health, and Happiness? 1992.*

☐ *Burn Rate: How I Survived the Gold Rush Years on the Internet._1998.*

☐ *Autumn of the Moguls: My Misadventures With the Titans, Poseurs, and Money Guys Who Mastered and Messed Up Big Media. 2003.*

- *The Man Who Owns the News: Inside the Secret World of Rupert Murdoch.* 2008.

- *Television Is the New Television: The Unexpected Triumph of Old Media In the Digital Age..* 2015.

- *Fire and Fury: Inside the Trump White House.* 2018.

Discussion Questions on Fire and Fury

1. Does the book seem to tell the truth or fabricate stuff?

2. What is the most shocking revelation in the book?

3. Would you recommend this book to others? Why or why not?

4. How has the book changed your view of Trump?

5. Who seems like the most qualified professional in the Trump administration in light of the text?

Do you want special deals?

Our mission is to bring you the highest quality companion books on the most popular books on the planet to enrich and heighten your reading experience like never before!

We frequently give out free books or 0.99 discounted promotions on Amazon.

Be in the loop and receive special notifications by subscribing to our SpeedyReads membership mailing list. By subscribing, you'll not only receive updates on the latest offer, you'll get "juicy" background information about novels you love, as well as a free copy of **"Delicious Reading: How**

to Quadruple and Enhance Your Book Reading Experience Within 24 Hours" report and video package.

Check out the link below to learn more:

http://www.easysummaries.com/gift to sign up to SpeedyReads Free Membership!

FINAL SURPRISE BONUS

Final words from the author…

Hope you've enjoyed this summary of Fire and Fury: Inside the Trump White House.

I always like to over-deliver, so I'd like to give you one final bonus.

Do me a favor, if you enjoyed this book, please leave a review on Amazon.

It'll help get the word out so more people can find out more about this special book!

If you do, I'll send you one of my most cherished collection report – Free:

Tantalizing Trivia Questions to Test Your IQ on Fire and Fury: Inside the Trump White House and Michael Wolff!

Here's how to claim your free report:

Leave a review on Amazon (longer the better but I'd be grateful for whatever length)

Enter your best email address here:
speedyreads24@gmail.com

Receive your free report – "**Tantalizing Trivia Questions to Test Your IQ on Fire and Fury:**

Inside the Trump White House and Michael Wolff!" – immediately!

Lightning Source UK Ltd.
Milton Keynes UK
UKHW020936121218
333833UK00001B/129/P